ART OF THE CALENDAR

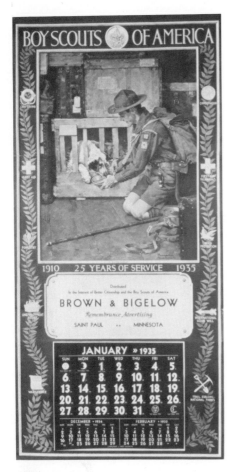

A GOOD SCOUT, 1935, by Norman Rockwell. Size: 22" × 46". This illustration is reproduced with permission of the Boy Scouts of America and copyright by Brown and Bigelow, St. Paul, Minn.

3·'27

GEN. 3:6

ART OF THE CALENDAR

BY MARK GABOR

Harmony Books

A division of Crown Publishers, Inc.
New York

Acknowledgments

I am most grateful for the support and cooperation of the staff at Brown & Bigelow, St. Paul, Minnesota. My thanks to Maurie Eichers for revealing the mystique of calendar art; to Ray Brand for the facts and figures; to Bill Bloedel for the marvelous anecdotes; and to Jim Patterson for the complete history of the world's largest calendar company.

I am indebted to Kathy Mack Kahn for assisting me through nearly a century of B & B's archived calendars; and to Alan Kahn for his guidance and hospitality during my dusty stay in Minnesota.

Special thanks to the English sources: Jim Wilson and J. R. Tabor, of Eversheds Ltd., St. Albans; and Ken Clark and Brian Rushton, of Bemrose & Sons Ltd., Derby.

On the continent, my thanks to Princesse Salm-Salm of Top Present, Munich, Germany; and to Werner Löenhardt of Antik Print, Amsterdam, Holland.

If it's possible to thank an institution — its facilities and staff — I am indebted to The New York Public Library.

Publisher: Bruce Harris
Editor: Linda Sunshine
Book and Cover Design: J-C Suares
Assoc. Editor: Nancy Crow
Production: Gene Conner, Murray Schwartz

Harmony Books

A division of Crown Publishers, Inc.
419 Park Avenue South
New York, New York 10016

Published simultaneously in Canada by General Publishing Company Limited
Printed in the United States of America

Library of Congress Cataloging in Publication Data:
Gabor, Mark, 1939—
    Art of the calendar.
    1. Calendar art.   I. Title.
NC1002.C3G32 1976   741.68   76-4084
ISBN 0-517-52540-2
ISBN 0-517-52541-0 pbk.

INTRODUCTION

The exact origin of the calendar is unknown. The earliest calendars were strictly utilitarian, serving religious and agricultural functions. Their primary purpose was to keep the gods in good humor. Therefore, it was the priests who created and maintained calendar systems to record the stars, the seasons, the times of religious festivals, and times for planting and harvesting. The word "calendar" originated later, during the Holy Roman Empire, from the Latin "calendarium," an account book or ledger literally intended for entering interest rates on loans and investments.

Not until the Middle Ages were calendars used for ornamentation. But throughout their history there have been many kinds of calendar devices, fascinating in themselves as curious objects: bundles of notched sticks; symbols carved into stones; piles of stones. American Indians painted time counts on buffalo hides. The Saxons had the clog, a four-sided stick of wood fitted with a ring and hung on a peg. This clog was notched along its four edges for every day of the year and was decorated with pagan symbols to identify the feast and holy days.

The first printed calendar is thought to have been made around A.D. 1438 by Johannes Nider, an astronomy professor at the University of Vienna. Carved into wooden blocks, then inked and pressed onto paper, the printed image was painstakingly produced. Even in this primitive period of printing, certain calendars were illustrated with distinctive symbols for each month.

Johannes Gutenberg capitalized on a growing demand for calendars in the mid-fifteenth century by producing several different kinds. His first attempt, a calendar for 1448, was printed like a hanging poster that could be tacked or pasted onto walls. For the sake of simplicity and efficiency, Gutenberg's unillustrated calendar noted only the conventional days, without marking any of the celebrated saints' days. When more-detailed information was demanded by the public, several calendars appeared in the form of bound, illustrated almanacs.

Following the industrial revolution and the subsequent development of mass printing, the calendar became a commercial vehicle for promotional purposes. The modern calendar was born. Its original use as a mere agenda took on the new, significant function of being illustrated advertising. At the turn of the twentieth century, businessmen, particularly in America, observed that almost everyone needed a calendar for personal and professional use. There was a mass, captive audience in calendar users, and thus a perfect opportunity to promote products, services, or corporate images.

The first commercial calendars were the year-at-a-glance type that were produced and sponsored by printers. Others, which might be called co-ops, carried several different business ads. In 1869 George L. Coburn of Hartford, Connecticut, obtained a patent on a new design for a wall calendar with a permanent back and a calendar pad. The pad of removable sheets was printed on both sides — January on one, February on the other, and so on — so that the sheets could be thrown away every two months. Coburn publicized his calendar for sale to bankers, insurance companies, and "businessmen of all classes." By the 1890s the business of selling calendar advertising and promotion was well on its way to a multi-million-dollar future.

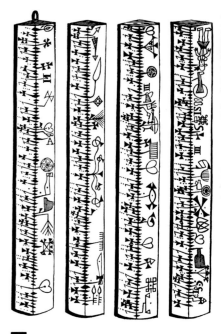

Early SAXON CLOG (circa sixth century A.D.) showing time interval notches and seasonal symbols. The clog is actually a single stick of wood. This line drawing is a composite showing all four sides.

Frontispiece: One of the latest additions to the retail calendar trade, Ballantine's M. C. ESCHER CALENDAR for 1976. Escher, a Dutch artist, is enjoying the same popularity that Rockwell and Parrish shared half a century ago. Escher's mind-boggling patterns and perspective games have replaced the pretty landscapes of the previous generation. Courtesy Ballantine Books, New York.

Because calendar production in the United States exceeds that of any other country, with more individual calendar makers than anywhere else, the modern history of the calendar—its form and content, its artists and commercial potential—is traced most easily through the history of the leading American producers. Today, hundreds of millions of calendars (mostly in color) are printed annually, and "businessmen of all classes" pay over two hundred fifty million dollars for this specific form of advertising.

Brown & Bigelow of St. Paul, Minnesota, is the world's largest calendar company, printing well over one hundred million calendars a year with worldwide distribution through licensees on five continents. Its many lines, from pocket size to poster size, covering hundreds of photographic and artist-rendered subjects from the trite to the fashionable, are calculated to fill every possible business and personal need. Their sales total around twenty million dollars annually, ample proof that they have a shrewd instinct for popular taste in design and variety.

One of Brown & Bigelow's first promotion pieces from 1904 explained the advertising potential of the calendar.

THE CHEAPEST

Method of advertising on earth is a good calendar. It combines a seasonable remembrance and souvenir with an all year's advertisement.

Let Us Suppose
that a banker, for instance, about holiday time would hand to each of his patrons a 5-cent piece or a dime with his compliments, half of them would throw the coin back to him and the other half would sneer at him as a very cheap fellow. But if, on the contrary, he should invest 5 or 10 cents in a genuine art calendar, he can please all comers at this trifling expense, and besides have his business sign displayed for 365 days in the home or office of the recipient of the calendar. Isn't it your honest judgment that the calendars shown in this book will accomplish all this?

Calendars issued by B & B in 1897 established certain subject themes that set the pattern for many calendar lines in years to come: children and animals, often in combination; landscapes and seascapes; pretty girls in portrait form or posed. But even with such traditional themes, calendar art represents a very special art form. The illustration must endure for at least a month and often for a year, but never longer. This distinguishes it from fine art, which is measured by its ability to last for centuries. Calendar art is more comparable to large, billboard advertising that must capture the viewer's interest in a passing glance and is soon replaced. Like the billboard, each calendar picture must tell a complete story, quite unlike book and magazine illustrations, which convey only a portion of the story.

Among B & B's early commissioned artists, the best known is probably Charles M. Russell, who is compared favorably today with Frederic Remington as being one of the finest "American West" artists. Russell was considered an unruly sort, a boozer and brawler, by many who knew him. He was poor for many years and often traded his paintings for liquor. In 1903 his business-minded wife Nancy took matters and paintings in hand, approached B & B, and sold the reproduction rights. At his peak, Russell's fee for a single work was fifteen thousand dollars. He died a rich man in 1927.

Around 1906, C. M. Coolidge started a line for the company based on a fantastic theme of poker-playing dogs. This immensely popular series has been reissued through the decades, even to the present. From 1906 to 1910 another popular artist, J. L. G. Ferris, did a patriotic, sentimental George Washington series.

The main body of early B & B calendars, however, consisted of single works by a seemingly endless number of anonymous artists. By 1915 the themes were expanded to attract an even wider range of the American business market. Family situations, country houses, classical pre-pinups, mother and child motifs, and situation comedies were added to the line.

Art Nouveau, which first became popular in commercial illustration at the turn of the century, did not appear on calendars until around 1918. There was a general trend, between 1915 and 1920, from the more traditional painterly modes to a flirtation with realism, impressionism, fashion style, and of course the popular Nouveau. These art styles could be found in B & B's increasingly diversified calendar line during this period. The twenties were rich years for B & B both financially and artistically, for in that decade, more than in any other, the

AZTEC CALENDAR STONE, or Rock of the Sun (circa 1481) in the National Museum, Mexico City. Made of basalt rock, the stone measures 11½ feet in diameter and weighs approximately 27 tons. This line drawing of the stone depicts the many symbols and time-counting systems carved on it.

Facing page: Dutch miniature ALMANACH/NADEN for the year 1634. Printed in Amsterdam, this almanac gave information about moon phases, holy days, tides, farming, and so on. The title page (top left) reads, "Small almanac after the new and old style, of the year 1634. Calculated by D. David Origa, Professor of the Elector of Brandenburg." The sample page (bottom left) depicts "Rulings of the moons in the Human Body . . . Aries rules the head, Taurus the neck, Gemini the arms . . ."

company succeeded in keeping up with the times, particularly the happy fashions of the Charleston era. Rolf Armstrong joined the B & B artists during this time and became one of the most innovative and famous "girl" artists to create for them. And in 1925 Norman Rockwell began his series of Boy Scout calendars that he continued for more than forty years, second in popularity and quantity only to his series of SATURDAY EVENING POST covers.

After Herbert Bigelow died in 1933, Brown & Bigelow was piloted by Charles Ward, a shrewd businessman under whose direction B & B introduced the multiple-sheet calendar featuring a different picture for each month, unlike the standard one-picture-per-year format. And new themes abounded in the thirties too. During this decade, Maxfield Parrish, already a well-established illustrator, began his outstanding line of landscapes for B & B, and Lawson Wood began to create his "humorous monkeys" group.

By World War Two, B & B was the largest, most-diversified calendar company in the world. Almost all the subject themes established by that time are still used today. Each year they are redone, updated somewhat, printed, packaged, and promoted a bit better than the year before. Generally, the art of the advertising calendar avoids controversy, espousing cuteness, light humor, God, country, family, and most recently, nostalgia. Brown & Bigelow's recent ecological series is probably successful because the illustrations are of animals, another traditional theme.

But subjects become standards partly because of the difficulties involved in production. Calendars must be printed a year before being sold. Therefore,

Title page from a bound, illustrated almanac for the year 1691, printed from woodblocks in Nuremburg, Germany. Literally translated, the title page reads, "Old and New Writing Calendar Of the Year After Jesus Christ's Birth 1691. Compiled with Diligence by Johann Christoph Wagner. Apart from monthly figures [there are] Health hints, Bloodletting charts, Marketfair days, Post-office information, Courier routes." Page size approximately 3" × 4½". Courtesy A. Korsch Verlag, Munich.

planning must begin two or three years prior to the date of use. Art directors must be able to anticipate future styles. Imagine a 1976 calendar showing an urban scene in which the newest car is from 1973. As a result of the time factor, many calendars, particularly advertising ones, are forced to be bland and nontopical.

From the 1920s, B & B's official company slogan was "Remembrance Advertising," reflecting the proven business concept that a free gift of a useful and attractive calendar is a "business builder"—another B & B motto. But sometime in the late sixties the company made an attempt to modernize its image; after forty years it was time for a change. In an effort to relate to contemporary advertising, they adopted two new slogans: "Motivational Communications" and "Imprint Media." The formidable B & B sales force went into the field to sell calendars, armed with new words and concepts from the home office. But they returned in defeat, because none of the clients understood what the slick new words meant. Before long B & B realized its mistake and, as no one had trouble understanding "Remembrance Advertising," it was officially reinstated as the firm's slogan in 1971–72.

Brown & Bigelow exports extensively to the entire world, but its largest foreign market is Europe. This may explain why European publishers have adopted American formulas and techniques within the calendar industry. There is practically no difference between European and American advertising calendars. The motifs are nearly identical; markets are similar. The one minor difference is that calendars from England, Germany, France, and Holland are usually more conservative than American ones. These publishers feel that their products are made with greater quality than their American counterparts. But with few exceptions, this claim seems exaggerated; the differences would be discernible only to professionals in the printing business. Yet, though the finest art calendars are produced abroad (especially in Germany and Switzerland), these are mostly retail rather than advertising items.

One of the largest English advertising calendar companies is Bemrose & Sons, Ltd., in Derby. Their advertising products division, Bemrose and Mansell, grosses over five million dollars annually. Established in 1926 as a general printer, Bemrose began publishing calendars in 1868 and advertised only their own services. It was not until 1908 that they started producing calendars with the imprints of other companies. Most Bemrose calendars feature reproductions of fine art from galleries and private collections around the world. Bemrose is particularly concerned with good taste in their artwork. They excel Brown & Bigelow in having less "cuteness," less storytelling, and virtually no overt patriotic themes. Still, their emphasis is also on reflecting the average person's appreciation of art by supplying quality illustrations that correspond to popular taste. Bemrose's best sellers are photographs of British and general scenic views, and the highly successful Mayfair pinup. The trend is nearly universal in England—the scenes outsell the girls.

Somewhat smaller than Bemrose is Evershed, Ltd., in St. Albans. Established as a family business in 1876, Evershed's was originally a small general printer serving the local tradesmen with blotters, posters, circulars, and of course calendars. There were no business imprints until the early 1900s when Evershed's applied stickers with the names of sponsoring companies to their calendars. Like Bemrose, Evershed's art has been largely drawn from English and Continental traditional masters as well as by occasionally commissioning artists for particular subjects.

The month of April from EN TAS ALMANACH, 1783. This Dutch miniature almanac included eclipses, portrait sketches of prominent people, and the opening and closing hours of the Port of Amsterdam. The poem under the illustration is a tribute to the Dutch naval hero Kinsbergen, "Kinsbergen who here shows himself/ He who inhabits a Hero's Soul/ Which he wants to devote to his country/ He is the delight of the Seafolks' life." Size: 1¼" × 2½".

Januar hat 31 Tage.

Allgem. Reichs-Kalender	Rußischer Kalender, December 1788.
1 D. Neujahr	21 Juliana
2 Fr. Abel, Seth	22 Anastasia
3 S. Enoch	23 10 Märtyrer in Cr.
4 S. S. n. Neujahr	24 29 S. n. Pf. Joh. I.
5 M. Simeon	25 Christtag
6 D. Heil 3 Könige	26 Verf. Maria
7 M. Julianus	27 Stephanus
8 D. Erhardus	28 20000 Märtyrer
9 Fr. Beatus	29 14000 Unsch. Kinder
10 S. Pauli Einsiedl.	30 Anysius
11 S. 1 Epiphan.	31 30 S. n. Pf. Luc. 2.
12 M. Reinholdus	1 Beschneid. Christi
13 D. Hilarius	2 Sylvester
14 M. Felix	2 Malachias
15 D. Maurus	4 Verf. 70 Apostel
16 Fr. Marcellus	5 Theopempt.
17 S. Antonius	6 Erschein. Christi
18 S. 2 Epiphan.	7 31 S. n. Pf. Luc. 2.
19 M. Sara	8 Georg
20 D. Fabian Sebast.	9 Polieuct.
21 M. Uanes	10 Gregorius
22 D. Vincentius	11 Theodosius
23 Fr. Emerentia	12 Tatiana
24 S. Timotheus	13 Ermilianus
25 S. 3 Epiphan. Pauli Bekehr.	14 32 S. n. Pf. Joh. 2.
26 M. Policarpus	15 Paulus
27 D. Chrisostomus	16 Petri Kettenfeier
28 M. Carolus	17 Antonius
29 D. Samuel	18 Athanas. Chr.
30 Fr. Adelgunda	19 Makarius
31 S. Virgilius	20 Euphemius

Januar 1789.

Eh bien ma poule, avez sans doute déjà un amoureux
Cecilie. T.I. pag. 190.
Nun mein Hündchen, schon ein Liebchen gehabt?
Cecilia I.T. s.

D. Chodowiecki fec.

Double page from 1789 German almanac featuring scenes from eighteenth-century plays. Here a lecherous gent says to the young lady, "Ah, well, my pet, without doubt you've already had a lover" (from the play CECILE). On the calendar page there are two kinds of listings. Left: The German Imperial Calendar for the month of January with all the saints' days. Right: A Russian calendar listing significant days such as "20,000 Martyrs Day" (Dec. 28), "14,000 Innocent Children's Day" (Dec. 29), and "Circumcision of Christ Day" (Jan. 1). Approximate size: 3" × 5". Courtesy A. Korsch Verlag, Munich.

In Germany there are dozens of large and small calendar companies. Many specialize in a particular kind of product. Most German wholesale calendars are not advertising calendars; they do not carry a company's imprint. The distinction between wholesale and retail in Germany is purely one of marketing. Therefore, the same products can be used for both retail and wholesale distribution, which is often solely to the export market.

Among the largest companies is A. Korsch Verlag, whose calendars first appeared in 1951 with a retail line, then in 1956 with a wholesale line. The firm's 1975 catalog carried approximately 115 titles with only one "girl" calendar, scenics and horses being their best sellers. Ackermanns Kunstverlag, another of Germany's large companies, has been issuing calendars for over one hundred years and specializes in fine art calendars, many of which cost more than twenty dollars each and are intended for art lovers and collectors. Top Present, started in 1965, is one of the most original calendar houses. Among their most-popular designs are an employee's morale calendar poking fun at the German work ethic and job situations in general, and "For Men Only," a datebook described as "hot stuff." The Multiverlages Company adds women to all the typical themes, even manufacturing calendars in which the traditional illustrations may be lifted to reveal a pinup beneath. Verlages Dr. Schwarze, a small firm, emphasizes reproductions of copper etchings and old lithographs intended particularly for hobbyists or collectors. One German company, Firma Gustav Winkler, makes calendars of pure cotton cloth, including a popular Walt Disney line. These few manufacturers described give some indication of the specialization and concern for international sales that distinguish German calendar publishing.

Unlike most calendar companies worldwide, modern Dutch printers rarely use artists. The manufacturers concentrate on high-quality photography and excel-

Almanac entitled "Order of Time, or Royal Calendar for 16 years," from 1694 through 1709. It contains pictures of royal figures, signs of the zodiac, names of the planets, sunrise and sunset times, and instructions on how to use the almanac.
Size: 6¼" × 8¼".

lence in printing. G. Kolff, one of Holland's big calendar publishers, was founded in 1848 and is one of the oldest calendar makers.

Remarkably, the popular French calendar differs from all others in that it is distributed by the postman and is neither a wholesale nor retail item. Long before the Christmas season, the postmen of France are supplied with catalogs and samples of calendar designs for the coming year. While making his daily rounds, the postman shows the material to those along his route and takes orders. He then purchases the finished calendars and gives them as gifts along with the regular mail during the following months. When he receives his holiday gratuity, it is invariably in excess of the cost of the calendar. This entire French market is virtually monopolized by a company called Editions Oberthur, which initiated the postman marketing idea in the mid-nineteenth century. This unusual method accounts for the calendar's French name, Almanach des P. T. T. (Poste et Telecommunication).

Although Europeans did manufacture nonadvertising calendars, the precedent for the retail calendar—one sold directly to the public—was most directly established by the pinup calendars evolving about the time of World War Two.

There were "girl" calendars in existence previously. The first known American one, issued by Brown & Bigelow, was entitled "Cosette." This charming but conservative portrait of a young beauty sold more than one and a half million calendars. In 1904 the first calendar in the alluring pinup style was also published by B & B. Once on the market, it proved that the "girlie" calendar would be a lucrative part of the business. The first calendar nude, "September Morn," a reproduction of an oil painting by the French artist Paul Chabas, appeared in 1913. It might have gone unnoticed in the United States if Anthony Comstock, of the New York Society for the Suppression of Vice, had not seen the work on display in a New York gallery window. Comstock demanded that the painting be removed. When a salesman explained that the painting had recently won a Medal of Honor from the French Academy, Comstock cried, "There's too little morn and too much maid! Take her out!" He and the other censors, however, were to fight a fierce but losing battle.

In 1933 ESQUIRE magazine published the Petty Girl and attracted an enormous following. By 1940 and the appearance of the Varga Girl, the girlie craze was gaining momentum. At that time the term "pinup" was coined. Though not originally produced as calendar illustrations, pinups were widely distributed to World War Two servicemen, not only in men's magazines but also in military entertainment publications. ESQUIRE decided, in the autumn of 1940, to capitalize on the popularity of Petty and Varga by publishing the first Varga Girl calendar. It featured twelve artist-rendered subjects, but with a photographic realism unlike any previous pinup types of calendars.

Shortly after its publication, ESQUIRE was taken to court by the U. S. Post Office concerning its second-class mailing privileges, considering the sexual nature of the Varga Girl. Following hearings in Washington, ESQUIRE was acquitted of the charges of publishing "lewd and lascivious" pictures. The pinup had gained more notoriety and was soon to become big business.

It was during these first pinup years that the most famous photographic pinup calendar of all was issued. In May 1949, Marilyn Monroe met Tom Kelley, a well-known California photographer, by accident. Having smashed up a friend's car on Sunset Boulevard, she needed taxi fare to get to a rehearsal on time. Kelley gave her five dollars and his business card. Several years later, apparently in

Title page from the first edition of POOR RICHARD'S ALMANACK, published by Benjamin Franklin in 1733. The title page lists year dates of other calendar systems. This almanac also contains "The lunations, Eclipses, Judgment of the weather, Spring Tides, Planet Motions & mutual Aspects, Sun and Moon Rising and Setting, Length of Days, Time of High Water, Fairs, Courts and observable Days."

need of money, she telephoned him and agreed to pose au naturel, which he had suggested once before. As the shutter snapped, Marilyn Monroe became Everyman's dream girl. She was paid fifty dollars. But the calendar sold in the millions, catapulting her name and image to national recognition and stardom.

PLAYBOY began publishing its familiar Playmate calendars in 1958 using only retouched photographs. This calendar was an instant success and is still extremely popular. Since the sixties, nearly every men's magazine has issued pinup calendars, each attempting sexier, bolder, or perhaps more elegant images than those initiated by PLAYBOY.

The large, independent calendar companies watched this mad scramble from a distance until 1971, when B & B issued their first pinup calendar, with a certain sense of humor. It was entitled "This Is A Plain Brown Wrapper," and contained a balanced mixture of nude and seminude models.

Unquestionably, the success of the pinup calendar gave impetus to the idea of selling other kinds of calendars directly to the public. As soon as other publishers in the late 1950s and 1960s realized the potential market, the retail calendar was established.

Because it is hung mainly for its aesthetic or educational value, the retail calendar is generally more fashionable, artistic, experimental, and of higher quality than the typical advertising calendar. Sold in bookstores, stationery shops, department stores, library and museum shops, and even art galleries, retail calendars are purchased overwhelmingly by women (for unknown reasons) and most often as gifts. They are relatively inexpensive compared to books of equivalent quality, and exhibit traditional and modern fine art and creative photography. The calendars are usually beautifully packaged, sometimes in expensive cardboard tubes, and are advertised as "the ideal gift for the New Year."

Publishers of retail calendars are from many different branches of the media world: greeting-card companies, book publishers, museums, libraries, magazines, and advertising calendar companies have begun to create separate retail lines. The themes, ranging from early Christian classics to the Pop movement, are as varied as the groups who produce these calendars.

Hallmark Cards, the leading firm in the mass-market, low-priced retail calendar business, focuses on art themes that, not surprisingly, are similar to their world-famous greeting-card lines. But though Hallmark may be the most successful single firm in the field, it seems that book publishers, taken collectively, also control a huge segment of the market.

Universe Books was the first of the book publishers to move into the calendar field. In 1957 they imported two art calendars from Germany and gradually expanded to include calendars from Switzerland, Austria, and Italy. In 1969 the company added its own U. S. calendars to their extensive line. The single most successful, and certainly most original, of Universe's calendars is "The Liberated Woman's Appointment Calendar," which was described by TIME magazine as being ". . . a compendium of feminist history, humor, sayings, and survival lore." Begun in 1970, its popularity has increased continually and now sells in the hundreds of thousands. The secret of Universe's success reflects the success of the retail calendar itself: it has dignified the calendar to the level of high-quality books. They have even been reviewed by critics and some have been distributed by a major book club.

Many other book publishers now issue retail calendars. Charles Scribner's

French political calendar, 1827, picturing representatives from both the right- and left-wing parties of the day. The calendar above the illustration lists only the holy and saints' days.

IMPERIAL CALENDAR, 1853, featuring Emperor Napoleon III, with verses dedicated to Louis-Napoleon Bonaparte, to France, and to Napoleon III. The calendar portion lists important holy days and all of the saints' days. Size: 8" × 10½".

PUNCH'S ALMANAC FOR 1856. Satiric caricatures of political figures in a parade winding through the year. One of the the themes, an urban complaint about the dirty water in the Thames River, could well be appropriate today. The calendar portion lists selected saints' days, the major holy days, and the birth and death dates of famous figures. Size: 7½" × 10".

Sons has a Sierra Club nature calendar and a large-format "Science Fiction Art Calendar." In 1973 Ballantine Books issued its first calendar, "The J. R. R. Tolkien Calendar," with holidays relating to life on Middle Earth based on Tolkien's famous trilogy THE LORD OF THE RINGS. In 1971 E. P. Dutton had instant success with their "Winnie the Pooh Calendar," using the original E. H. Shepard drawings. Simon & Schuster started late with "The Rod McKuen Calendar" for 1974. Of course, there are more book publishers, too numerous to discuss here, now involved in calendar marketing.

Museums publish and sell calendars, usually through their own shops, but sometimes distributing them to other outlets. There are perhaps only seven or eight museums and libraries in the United States that issue calendars. The two most prominent are The Museum of Modern Art in New York, which has produced calendars since 1957, and The Metropolitan Museum of New York, which has been publishing calendars since 1922.

Some of the larger advertising calendar companies have started separate retail lines in an effort to keep up with this expanding, profitable market. In 1971 Brown & Bigelow started a retail division, but the company's established conservatism may prove to be a difficulty for them in the competitive, contemporary retail market.

It is unfortunate that this study must conclude with the observation that the golden age of calendar art ended before 1950. Historically, the art of the calendar was most affected by the transition from the artist to the photographer. In the early years, from the late nineteenth century to the 1940s, artist-rendered calendars often characterized the eras to which they belonged, providing a kind of sociology of the decades.

Calendars could never be as modern as commercial illustration, nor, for the most part, compare favorably with fashion art, magazine illustration, even ordinary space advertising. The business community would not allow it, and the calendar companies, part of that conservative world and all too happy to "give 'em what they want," did not try, like other printed media, to influence or perhaps educate an audience that numbered in the hundreds of millions.

So there has been a conspicuous absence in calendars of minority views, not in the political, social, or economic sense, but rather, artistically, culturally, and intellectually. The important potential for artistic breakthrough lies in the obvious vitality and growth of the retail calendar and its inevitable influence on the commercial calendar.

Hopefully, the large advertising calendar companies will, as a result of competition, move in more creative directions. For the public deserves the finest possible art, the kind presented here, selected from many hundreds of excellent examples. These examples, however, are in the minority, exceptions in traditional calendar illustration.

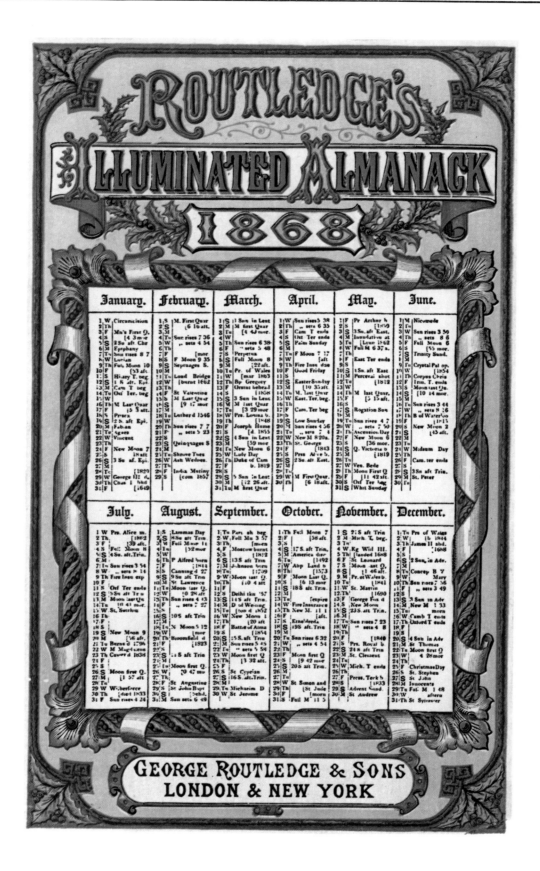

ROUTLEDGE'S ILLUMINATED AL-
MANACK, 1868. Published in London
and probably distributed in America also,
this decorative almanac was printed in five
colors and lists dates of major past events
such as the day "London Bridge Burnt,
1662" and the day "Orsini Beheaded,
1858." Size: 5" × 8¼".

This remarkable 1897 calendar was issued by the Antikamnia Chemical Company of St. Louis. Apparently, this pharmaceutical company was advertising a new drug called "Antikamnia, a coal-tar product." Taken in conjunction with codeine, the drug was a "nervous quiet-ant," and taken with quinine it could "control the tenacious and bloody character of pulmonary engorgement and inflammation." The drug was also said to relieve "fermentative dyspepsia . . . eruptation of gas, flatus and pum . . . duodenal catarrh . . . catarrhal jaundice . . . diarrhea . . . dysentery, cholera and typhoid fever."

The use of incongruous, if slightly fantastic, visual images was not uncommon in the early days of commercial illustration. Here the combination of skeleton figures in ordinary situations lends a morbid but humorous quality to the calendar. The art was rendered in 1896 by "L. Frusius," possibly a pseudonym, as there is no traceable record of this name in the art or illustration field. Printed by lithography by G. H. Buek & Co., New York. Size: 7" × 10".

Not a true almanac in the traditional sense, this 1881 English calendar begins to reflect a greater emphasis on artwork and quality reproduction. This painting is by A. E. Mulready (1876), and was printed by lithography in twelve colors.

The theme tells a story of two children lost in the rain. In the upper left corner of the painting, a poster offers a reward for "lost or stolen" children. Courtesy Bemrose & Sons, Derby.

"A Christmas Greeting"

ORIGINAL OIL PAINTING.

This marvelous 1905 English calendar was produced in Leeds by Alf Cooke, "Her Majesty's Color Printer." Entitled A CHRISTMAS GREETING and executed in the style of the French posterists at the turn of the century, the picture emphasizes the good life (bicycles were the rage then) and the cheer and gaiety of the Christmas holidays. Printed in "Gold and 14 Colours," each color was painstakingly hand-drawn with lithographic chalk on grained stones. Courtesy Bemrose & Sons, Derby.

These are the famous poker-playing dogs by C. M. Coolidge, a milestone in calendar art. Coolidge's special gift was in conveying a complete range of human expressions through canine features. The series was first issued in 1906, but has remained in print and popular to the present time. Size: 14" × 9½". Courtesy Brown & Bigelow.

THE RESCUE, 1935. Left: A calendar commemorating the disabled American veterans of World War I, by J. O. Todahl. The dramatic picture is described as "Action and color and light; the grim reality of a high moment of sacrifice gladly offered." Size: 9" × 11". Courtesy Brown & Bigelow. Right: A determined Uncle Sam stands amidst wartime symbols of America's industrial strength. Patriotism was high from the late 1930s through World War II. Many calendars such as this 1940 example were successfully distributed. Artist unknown. Size: 9¾" × 11¼". Courtesy Brown & Bigelow.

THE LADY OF THE NILE

BROWN & BIGELOW
Remembrance Advertising
ST. PAUL, MINN.   SAULT STE. MARIE, ONT.

Left: THE LADY OF THE NILE, a 1925 calendar picturing an exotic pinup resting seductively in a moonlit Egyptian setting. Based on classic poses of reclining figures, this illustration is characteristic of the kind of gimmick used to make a respectable pinup. Artist unknown. Size: 15½″ × 20″. Courtesy Brown & Bigelow.

A delightful English calendar for 1932, entitled JEALOUSY: A STUDY FROM LIFE. The theme seems a bit irrelevant when compared with the skillful artistic treatment, the poise of the model, and the very fashionable hairdo, dress, and shoes. Artist's name illegible. Size: 6″ × 10″. Courtesy Bemrose & Sons, Derby.

The famous Varga calendars were published by ESQUIRE magazine and were extremely popular. Sharp as a color photo, the "Varga Girl" was queen of the artist-rendered calendar pinups—with annual distribution exceeding the million mark as early as 1942. These calendars began a whole trend in pinup publishing that was exploited in the 1950s by PLAYBOY magazine, publisher of the "Varga Girl" after the artist left ESQUIRE in 1946. Size: 12" × 9".

Horses and women have been a successful duo on hundreds of calendars through the years. In this example, the theme of the American Indian Girl adds additional appeal to the fundamentally pinup image. Courtesy Brown & Bigelow.

Seymour Chwast and Milton Glaser of Push Pin Studios designed this calendar for 1975 as a promotion for the Pepsi-Cola Company. The calendar is six feet long and printed on both sides. Drawings for the calendar were done by Chwast, Glaser, Haruo Miyauchi, Christian Piper, George Stavrinos and Doug Gervasi. Although this calendar was produced as a premium giveaway, it has the look and appeal of a retail calendar.

The next three calendars reflect the popular taste of late-nineteenth-century England. Although the basic themes were similar to America's during that era, the stylistic treatments were decidedly English. The 1889 calendar pictured below has the winning combination of children and the seaside. The 1892 example at the bottom of page 36 is an early photographic landscape printed by collotype, a lithographic process. The 1897 calendar at the top of page 36 portrays a demure country girl. Courtesy Bemrose & Sons, Derby.

In this delicate 1900 calendar, reproduced here actual size, Colgate & Company promotes its line of toiletries. Each month is illustrated with detailed color engravings of various birds. Pocket calendars were not uncommon at this time, though most were in the form of almanacs and contained general information. This example has a simple calendar promoting only one company. Printed by the Forbes Co., Boston.

MORE MONEY IN HOSIERY THAN BANKS

Calendar art with a moral: "More Money in Hosiery Than in Banks." This piece stresses the danger of not banking one's money, and was probably designed as a bank calendar. The painting by Bownen was executed around 1900 and re-produced on a Brown & Bigelow calendar in 1902. Note the pseudoseductive pose of the woman and the mysterious shadow behind the robber. Size: 11¾" × 9¼". Courtesy Brown & Bigelow.

Black child, circa 1906, in a picture entitled "The Bottomless Pit," referring to the child's stomach, though today we might think it meant her ghettolike surroundings. Ironically, humor was the intention of this unflattering study. But now such a subject would be considered taboo, unless done satirically, as in the illustration on page 122. Size: 4½" × 6". Artist unknown. Courtesy Brown & Bigelow.

NOVEMBER, 1909

SUN	MON	TUE	WED	THR	FRI	SAT
	1	2	3	4	5	6
7	8	9	10	11	12	13
14	15	16	17	18	19	20
21	22	23	24	25	26	27
28	29	30	Last Quar. 4th	New Moon 12th	First Quar. 20th	Full Moon 27th

This familiar portrait of GENERAL WASHINGTON was painted in 1907 by J. L. G. Ferris, one of Brown & Bigelow's more famous artists during the company's early years. The general first appeared on the 1909 calendar shown here. This calendar was printed specifically for the Pawtucket Mutual Fire Insurance Company and distributed from Massachusetts. Size: 11" × 17". Courtesy Brown & Bigelow.

40

A superb 1913 showcase of American patriotism displaying some of the best techniques of commercial illustration. Perched high on a steel girder, the figure attaches the Stars and Stripes while other flags are flying high from the tops of New York City skyscrapers. This symbolic gesture of American growth and strength suggests victory, as though the figure were implanting a flag at the top of a newly conquered mountain. The composition is strong—as are the colors in the foreground, contrasting with its pale sky. Size: 11″ × 16″. Artist unknown. Courtesy Brown & Bigelow.

J. L. G. Ferris's interpretation of Gilbert Stuart at work on the most famous portrait of Washington—the one appearing in reverse on the dollar bill. Not without a sense of humor, Ferris depicts Martha Washington giving a chatty critique on Stuart's portrait. Courtesy Brown & Bigelow.

This slightly damaged antique calendar was painted in 1910 by Robert Robinson and is called HONEST. The script in the upper left corner reads, "Compliments of Royal Stock Food Co., by Uncle Sam." On its right side is a glued-on photograph, possibly of the model or the artist or perhaps both. The art reflects the honesty and reliability both of old age and the company it represents. Size: 11″ × 15″.

A colorful child-fantasy by Frances Tipton Hunter, 1929. Reproduced from an original watercolor, the illustration sets the doll-like figure in an imaginary world of dense flowers and magic bubbles, one containing a sprite with a wand. The picture is sheer escapist, similar to the psychedelic art that followed many years later. Size: 6½" × 8½". Courtesy Brown & Bigelow.

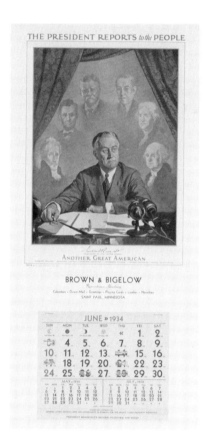

This 1934 calendar shows Franklin D. Roosevelt during his first term as President. The shadowy figures in the background are Andrew Jackson, Abraham Lincoln, Theodore Roosevelt, Woodrow Wilson, Thomas Jefferson, and George Washington. Artist, G. Krollmann. Courtesy Brown & Bigelow.

BE AMERICAN—BUY AMERICAN, a 1934 depression calendar urging us to "join the Made-in-America club" by purchasing only American-made products instead of "inferior foreign-made goods . . . from cheap foreign labor." The illustration has a pop-art quality in the bold center emblem. The background portrays industry, transportation, the Capitol, and a rainbow, all symbolizing optimism. Artist unknown. Size: 10" × 12". Courtesy Brown & Bigelow.

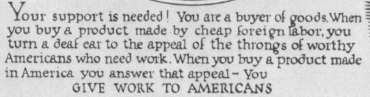

Your support is needed! You are a buyer of goods. When you buy a product made by cheap foreign labor, you turn a deaf ear to the appeal of the throngs of worthy Americans who need work. When you buy a product made in America you answer that appeal—You
GIVE WORK TO AMERICANS

AMERICA MARCHES ON, a 1935 inspirational calendar. "Progress," says the headline, "is the activity of today and the assurance of tomorrow." The message is clear—onward with prosperity—and the background airplanes were common symbols of American growth in the 1930s. The artist is Edward M. Eggleston, a popular calendar producer for Brown & Bigelow. Size: 11" × 16".

NESTOR 6331

BROWN & BIGELOW

Remembrance Advertising

SAINT PAUL, MINNESOTA

JANUARY » 1935

SUN	MON	TUE	WED	THU	FRI	SAT
		1	2	3	4	5
6	7	8	9	10	11	12
13	14	15	16	17	18	19
20	21	22	23	24	25	26
27	28	29	30	31		

DECEMBER • 1934

FEBRUARY • 1935

A safety calendar for 1934, issued by Brown & Bigelow as one in a long-continuing series of such promotions. The artwork in this excellent example appears to have been rendered by two artists—one for the foreground and bordering safety-insets, the other for the scenic background. Calendars of this kind were designed specifically for service stations and were distributed extensively across the country. Artist unknown. Size: 16" × 33".

Postage-stamp art from a White & Wyckoff calendar of 1935. The artwork on each of the twelve months was from a different foreign postage stamp. On the back of each month, a column entitled "The Romance of Stamps" provided lengthy explanations for each stamp. For February (right) a Mongolian stamp depicts the capture of a wild horse. According to the text, the Mongolian people ". . . literally live and grow on horses . . . and while the Arabian horse is most famous, the Arab is second to the Mongol when it comes to riding." The Spanish stamp (below) portrays The Christ of the Andes, a monument erected on the Andean border between Chile and Argentina. White & Wyckoff started its "Romance of Stamps" calendar series in 1905. Artist unknown. Size: 10" × 15".

A rare commercial calendar (1937), in the streamline tradition of Art Deco. The calendar promotes the use of the new light metal, aluminum. Artist unknown. Size: 8½″ × 12″.

PROGRESS: Railroads needed faster trains...so turned to streamlining...chose aluminum alloys as the ideal material because of lightness, strength and easy workability.

1937	MARCH					1937
S	M	T	W	T	F	S
	1	2	3	4	5	6
7	8	9	10	11	12	13
14	15	16	17	18	19	20
21	22	23	24	25	26	27
28	29	30	31			

1937		APRIL				1937
SUN.	MON.	TUES.	WED.	THURS.	FRI.	SAT.
				1	2	3
4	5	6	7	8	9	10
11	12	13	14	15	16	17
18	19	20	21	22	23	24
25	26	27	28	29	30	

1937	MAY					1937
S	M	T	W	T	F	S
						1
2	3	4	5	6	7	8
9	10	11	12	13	14	15
16	17	18	19	20	21	22
23/30	24/31	25	26	27	28	29

ALCOA ALUMINUM IN STOCK READY FOR IMMEDIATE DELIVERY

ALCOA ALUMINUM

WHITEHEAD METAL PRODUCTS COMPANY of New York, Inc.
304-314 Hudson Street • NEW YORK, N. Y.

Distributors of Metals   WALKER 5-4500   *Distributors of Metals*

TOWARD THE LIGHT, inspiration for 1939—the haunting image of a World War I soldier and a courageous-looking father and son walking toward peace. World War II was just down the road. An accompanying poem refers to the First World War "just twenty-one years ago" and says, "There's a long, long trail a-winding/ Since our throats were clutched by gas/ Since Yank and Frenchie/ Heinie, too/ Sobbed out: 'They shall not pass!' . . . We who know that long trail's horror/ With Machine guns at each bend/ Must keep our sons straight toward the light/ Of a peace that must not end." Artist, H. M. Stoops. Size: 8½" × 11". Courtesy Brown & Bigelow.

An English calendar book, 1936, celebrating the style of PUNCH MAGAZINE. Right: The title page, featuring the August 17, 1927, cover of PUNCH. Below: A sample cartoon from this series, displaying typical English humor but lacking the spirit of the original PUNCH. Published by G. Delgado, Ltd., London. Size: 7″ × 9½″.

She. "Isn't it funny? As a rule dogs hate music. Tootles seems to love it."
He. "Perhaps he thinks it's something else."

For many years, "Ripley's Believe It or Not!" was issued in calendar format by Brown & Bigelow. Of special interest for calendar art is this 1940 item concerning George and Martha Washington that refers to the introduction of the Gregorian calendar system to America in 1752. Size: 16" × 24½".

THE BEST THAT MONEY CAN BUY

B&B GAS
OILS
GREASES

GAS

Buckwheat   Mickey   Darla   Alfalfa   Porky

OUR GANG

"The Big Shot"

PARK GARAGE & SERVICE STATION

Complete One-Stop Service

Gasoline	T. M. JONES, Prop.	Batteries
Oils	Nestor 6331	Tires
Greasing		Washing

HANS GROENHOFF

Beechcraft 35

Above: A marvelous (but improbable) photograph of American status symbols. Photographer Hans Groenhoff creates an elegant suburban scene while advertising the Beechcraft 35 airplane. The postwar period of prosperity began in 1947, and it would be hard to imagine a more revealing picture of the American dream at that time. Every detail is included here: the neatly manicured landscaping, the latest clothing, automobiles, luggage, golf bags, and, of course, the national flag. The flaw is in the shadows. Size: 13½" × 16½".

A WINNING COMBINATION, 1946 (right), one of Rolf Armstrong's most colorful paintings, showcasing patriotism and the all-American girl. Behind her "float the glorious colors of our gallant allies." Size: 12" × 22½". Courtesy Brown & Bigelow.

MAXFIELD PARRISH & NORMAN ROCKWELL

Maxfield Parrish was one of the most famous illustrators to execute a long series of calendars on a specific theme— landscapes. In the 1930s, Parrish was well known for his prints, magazine covers, illustrated children's books (especially THE ARABIAN NIGHTS and THE CHILD'S GARDEN OF VERSES), and his two magnificent murals—"Old King Cole," in New York's St. Regis Hotel, and "The Pied Piper," in San Francisco's Sheraton Palace Hotel.

He was commissioned by Brown & Bigelow in 1936, at the age of sixty-six. Many people wrongly assumed that Parrish had passed his peak as an artist, and no one could have guessed that he had thirty years ahead of him to produce three decades of calendars.

The B & B commission was ideal for Parrish at that time in his life, because he could peacefully depict the rural New England serenity in which he lived, and he could illustrate the deep reverence he had for nature. (He was once quoted as saying, "A tree is a nobler object than a prince in his coronation robes.")

Only Parrish could have created the special aura of peace and solitude that is so apparent in these calendars. His technique was greatly influenced by his father's etchings, by his abiding interest in architecture, and by his study of the Old Masters. In his landscapes one sees a blending of these influences: the etcher, in the careful delineation of each leaf and shadow; the architect, in the symmetry of his buildings; and the Old World craftsman, in the painstaking technique that lends richness to the unmistakable

"Parrish colors." He used unmixed transparent paints (rather than opaque oils) in the form of glazes painted on a pure white background. He painted layer over layer to build depth and intensity, and in this way preserved the purity of color as it came out of the tube.

The Parrish landscapes are among the best calendar illustrations ever created. They are not merely scenics; they transcend this calendar genre, reaching a level of holy appreciation for the serenity, wonder, and magic of nature.

All the Parrish calendars are courtesy of the Maxfield Parrish Estate and Brown & Bigelow.

Left: The Calendar of Cheer, 1923.
Right: The Calendar of Friendship, 1925.

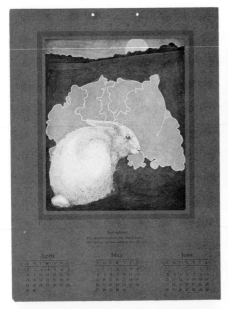

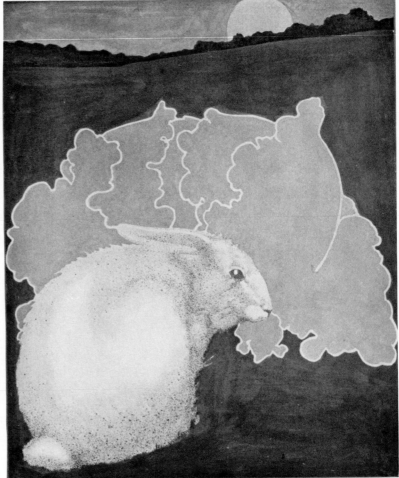

These illustrations, from a rare 1906 Parrish calendar, are collector's items. They show the taste, style, and execution upon which the artist's early reputation was built. One sees how readily Parrish's work lent itself to children's book illustration, and why the artist was considered unique—if not inspired—during this early period. Unidentified calendar from a private collection.

QUIET SOLITUDE   MAXFIELD PARRISH

BROWN & BIGELOW

Remembrance Advertising

B▷◁B

CALENDAR FRANCHISES   DISTINCTIVE BUSINESS GREETINGS   DELUXE LEATHER GOODS
DIRECT MAIL CAMPAIGNS   ADVERTISING PLAYING CARDS   METAL, PLASTIC SPECIALTIES

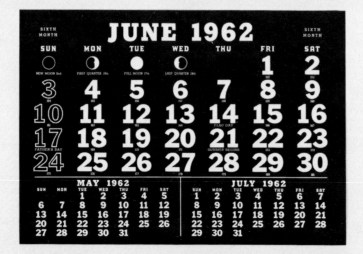

From 1925 to 1975, Norman Rockwell produced the Boy Scout calendars, one of his largest series of illustrations on a single theme. Brown & Bigelow commissioned his paintings under an exclusive authorization from the Boy Scouts of America. The illustrations on the following pages—selected from the entire series—are characteristic examples of Rockwell's treatment of this patriotic and sometimes religious theme.

Rockwell's stylistic development from decade to decade is apparent in these calendars. At first the art was soft edged and expressionistic. By 1940 he had evolved the almost photographic crispness and detail that constitute the famous Rockwell style. In the late 1960s his technique changed again, to seem oddly reminiscent of the softer style of the very earliest Boy Scout calendars.

For twenty years (from 1950 to 1970), Rockwell also produced his familiar Four Seasons calendar series. In each he portrayed humorous human-interest situations, using the same characters throughout each individual calendar. Rockwell's own words, appearing on a 1952 calendar, best describe this series:

Spring, Summer, Fall, Winter—I've no favorite. To me all the garbs of nature are wonderful and beautiful and each season has its own precious personal recollections, nostalgic memories of little everyday incidents out of the past that grow in importance with the passing of time. . . . These simple scenes represent to me some of the glory and wonder of nature, a little of the joy and happiness of freedom, and a whole lot of the just plain goodness of living.

A year later he wrote that "I've enjoyed painting these pictures . . . [they] seem to typify a friendly way of life—the best way—our American way."

During his long association with Brown & Bigelow, Rockwell also produced several "one-shot" calendars, those not a part of either series. "It's Your Move" (right) is one of his finest individual calendars. As an entire collection, Rockwell's work represents some of the best art in the history of commercial calendars.

BROWN & BIGELOW

"The Girl of my Dreams" (1931)

House of Quality

BROWN & BIGELOW

Remembrance Advertising
REG. U.S. PAT. OFF.

1932	JANUARY				1932	
SUN	MON	TUE	WED	THU	FRI	SAT
New Moon 7th	First Quar. 15th	Full Moon 23rd	Last Quar. 30th		1	2
3	4	5	6	7	8	9
10	11	12	13	14	15	16
17	18	19	20	21	22	23
24/31	25	26	27	28	29	30

1931	DECEMBER				1931		1932	FEBRUARY				1932	
SUN	MON	TUE	WED	THU	FRI	SAT	SUN	MON	TUE	WED	THU	FRI	SAT
		1	2	3	4	5		1	2	3	4	5	6
6	7	8	9	10	11	12	7	8	9	10	11	12	13
13	14	15	16	17	18	19	14	15	16	17	18	19	20
20	21	22	23	24	25	26	21	22	23	24	25	26	27
27	28	29	30	31			28	29					

SAINT PAUL, MINNESOTA

MEXICO CITY, MEXICO   SAULT STE. MARIE, ONTARIO   HAVANA, CUBA

BOY SCOUTS OF AMERICA

A SCOUT IS HELPFUL

He must be prepared at any time to save life, help injured persons, and share the home duties. He must do at least one "Good Turn" to somebody every day.
(The Third Scout Law.)

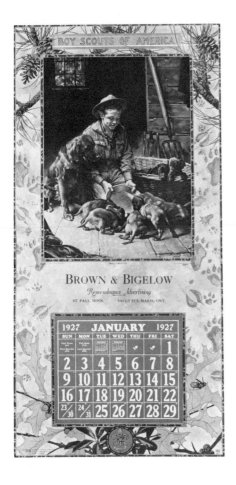

"1927"
This illustration reproduced with permission of the Boy Scouts of America and copyright by Brown & Bigelow, St. Paul, Minn.

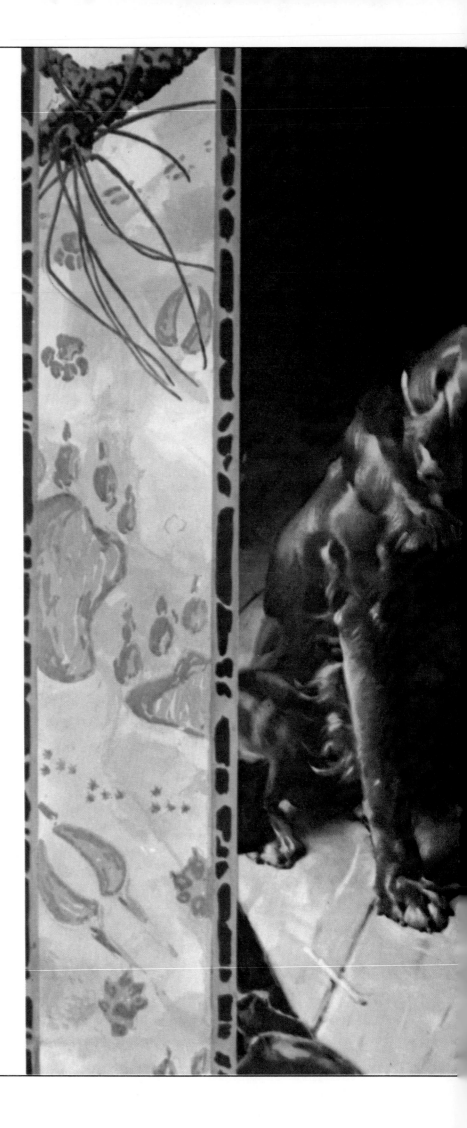

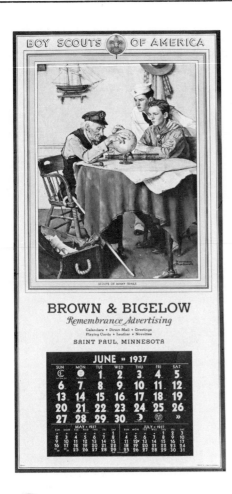

"**S**couts of Many Trails" (1937)
This illustration reproduced with permission of the Boy Scouts of America and copyright by Brown & Bigelow, St. Paul, Minn.

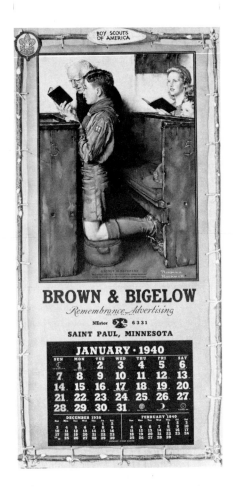

"**A** Scout Is Reverent" (1940)
This illustration reproduced with permission of the Boy Scouts of America and copyright by Brown & Bigelow, St. Paul, Minn.

"**G**rowth of a Leader"
This illustration reproduced with permission of the Boy Scouts of America and copyright by Brown & Bigelow, St. Paul, Minn.

"1963"
This illustration reproduced with permission of the Boy Scouts of America and copyright by Brown & Bigelow, St. Paul, Minn.

ummer 1950"

"**S**pring 1950"

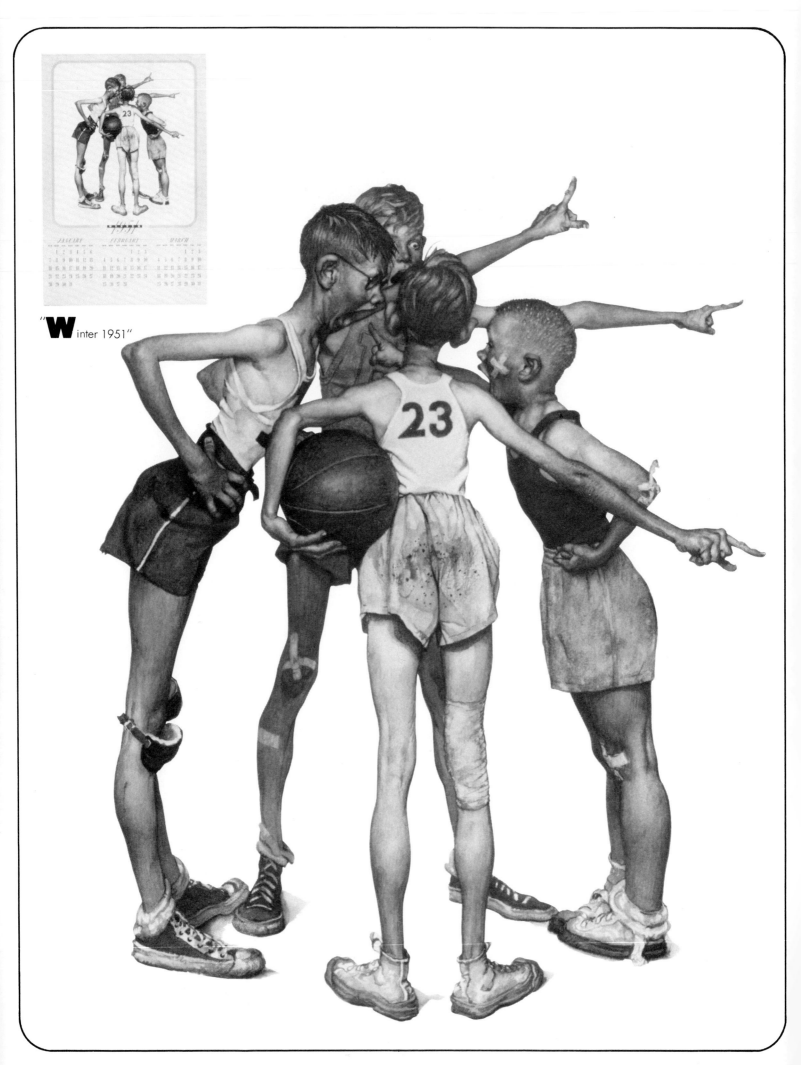

"**W**inter 1951"

84

"**S**pring 1955"

"**W**inter 1957"

"**S**pring 1963"

Norman
Rockwell

BROWN & BIGELOW

ST. PAUL 4 ⊠ Remembrance Advertising ⊠ MINNESOTA

JANUARY	FEBRUARY	MARCH
s m t w t f s	s m t w t f s	s m t w t f s
1	1 2 3 4 5	1 2 3 4 5
2 3 4 5 6 7 8	6 7 8 9 10 11 12	6 7 8 9 10 11 12
9 10 11 12 13 14 15	13 14 15 16 17 18 19	13 14 15 16 17 18 19
16 17 18 19 20 21 22	20 21 22 23 24 25 26	20 21 22 23 24 25 26
23 30 24 31 25 26 27 28 29	27 28	27 28 29 30 31

"**W**inter 1966"

BROWN & BIGELOW

"**S**ummer 1970"

"**S**pring 1970"

Almost from the beginnings of American calendar art, the "Western" was a leading seller. IN WITHOUT KNOCK-ING (1909) was painted by Charles M. Russell, the well-known cowboy artist, who made his reputation in calendars. Many artists followed Russell in portraying Western scenes, but none seemed to capture so well the critical action, that right moment of so many different cowboy scenes. Size: 14" × 11½". Courtesy Brown & Bigelow.

Another Western scene by Charles M. Russell used, quite appropriately, to promote Remington firearms and ammunition. The weaponry is noticeably highlighted in this picture. Size: 16½" × 21". Courtesy Brown & Bigelow.

Philip R. Goodwin, another of Brown & Bigelow's early masters, became famous for his portrayals of American frontier life. As shown here in TWO'S COMPANY (ca. 1910), Goodwin focused on the pioneering woodsmen called "cruisers," who penetrated the deep, trackless forests of North America, charting the land, observing the wildlife, surviving on their prowess and resourcefulness. Goodwin, who once studied under the famed illustrator Howard Pyle, eventually lived the outdoor life himself, armed mainly with a sketchpad. He brought to civilization—and to literally millions of people—unforgettable scenes of life and survival in the wilds. Public interest in Goodwin's work has never slackened, and Brown & Bigelow has successfully reissued almost all the works he was originally commissioned to do in the early part of the century. Goodwin's forte was in capturing the special qualities of his outdoor heroes—their ruggedness, calm, strength, silence, independence, and respect for the great woodlands. Size: 18" × 28".

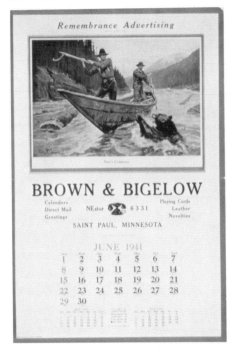

Fragrant as the Great Outdoors

In this splendid example of 1920s commercial illustration, artist Oliver Kemp portrays a lush, romantic outdoors scene that depicts the association between nature and a fragrant tobacco. Commissioned exclusively for the Forest Stream Tobacco Company, this calendar exemplifies the soft-sell approach to promoting a specific product. Previously, a product was never included in the artwork itself.

The figures here seem a bit awkward anatomically. Neither one appears to be looking at the fishing line, and one wonders where the man's arm ends. Oddly enough, these incongruities add to the charm of the picture, and one is taken with the warm colors and serenity of the scene. Size: 13" × 19". Courtesy Brown & Bigelow.

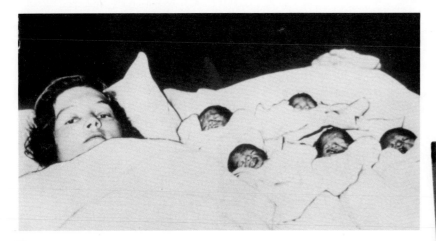

ne of Brown & Bigelow's most un-usual (and quite successful) series featured the Dionne quintuplets from infancy through their twenty-first year. The series lasted from 1935 to 1956, when one of the quints died and the public lost interest in them. The artwork was done by Andrew Loomis.

Brown & Bigelow tried a new series in the 1950s with the Fischer quintuplets, but the market had obviously changed in twenty years. The new series was unsuc-cessful and was discontinued almost im-mediately.

THE DIONNE QUINTUPLETS
MARIE   YVONNE   ANNETTE   CECILE
BORN IN CALLANDER, ONTARIO, CANADA MAY 28, 1934

1936

1936

1937

1938

1941

1942

1943

1944

1948

1949

1950

1952

1956

BROWN & BIGELOW

Remembrance Advertising

SAINT PAUL 4, MINNESOTA

With Compliments from
FRED. H. OSBORNE
BAKER AND CONFECTIONER
STATION ROAD, SHERINGHAM
TELEPHONE: SHERINGHAM 264

Calendar

GRACE
39

The JACK CALENDAR FOR 1941, featuring sailor, mascot (both cut out and raised from cardboard backing), and a British flag—a rare example of English patriotism in calendars. Owing to paper shortages in England during World War II, this calendar publisher was forced to print on the same cardboard used for milk-bottle tops during that period. Thus occurred the possibility of die-cutting the cardboard to create a three-dimensional image. Artist, A. L. Grace. Size: 6½" × 8". Courtesy Eversheds Ltd., St. Albans.

These two royal photographs were used quite successfully on many of Eversheds' calendars. They are H. R. H. Prince Charles (right), 1954, and H. R. H. Princess Elizabeth (below), 1952. Affixed to the prince's calendar was the following copy: "Heir to the throne: Unaware of the responsibilities that lie ahead of him, Prince Charles has already won all hearts with his unaffected good manners, playfulness and boyish high spirits. In his quieter moods he gives evidence of a grave dignity and thoughtfulness towards others which is rare in one so young. This delightful study brilliantly captures his princely charms." Portrait of Prince Charles by the noted photographer Marcus Adams. Size: 6½" × 8½". The photographer of Princess Elizabeth is unidentified. Size: 7¼" × 8¼". Courtesy Eversheds Ltd., St. Albans.

H.R.H. PRINCE CHARLES

SEPTEMBER MORN, the first-known nude calendar girl. Millions of pirated copies of "Matinée Septembre," an oil painting by Paul Chabas, appeared on calendars from about 1913. Courtesy Universe Books, New York.

LAUGHING WATER

A "girl" calendar with an American Indian theme, LAUGHING WATER (1935), is somewhat unusual for its full nudity. Artist unknown. Size: 5" × 7". Courtesy Brown & Bigelow.

An alluring pinup calendar, GOLDEN HOURS (1936), by the well-known "girl" artist Earl Moran. The model is scantily clad in a sheer blue swimsuit, and stares directly at the viewer. Moran was a leading fashion illustrator before working for Brown & Bigelow. He studied previously at the Chicago Art Institute and the Art Students' League in New York. He became one of B & B's most successful pinup artists. Size: 4" × 7".

Two seductive portraits of women from
Brown & Bigelow's famous artists. Left:
"Thinking of You," by Rolf Armstrong,
1932. Right: "Show Girl," a shadowy
pinup by Earl Moran, 1940.

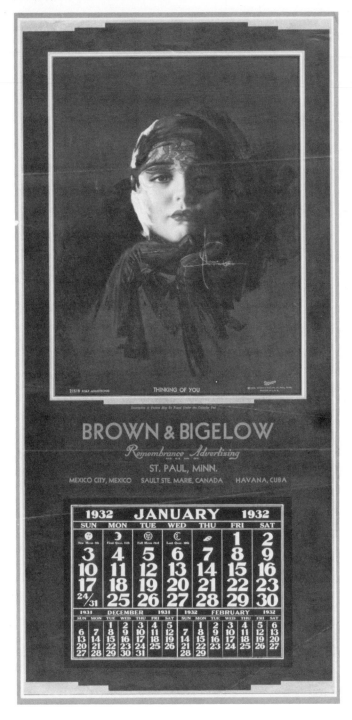

MIMI, a charming and sophisticated
calendar, 1933, contains hints of both Art
Nouveau and Art Deco—the former in the
patterns and colors of the model and pil-
lows, the latter in the blue frame around
the picture and the design of the date pad.
The composition, particularly because of
all the blank space around the painted
(watercolor and ink) forms, is beautifully
balanced, elegant, and graceful—in
harmony with the flowing gesture of the
model toying lazily with a cat. Artist unknown. Size: 10¼" × 14". Courtesy
Brown & Bigelow.

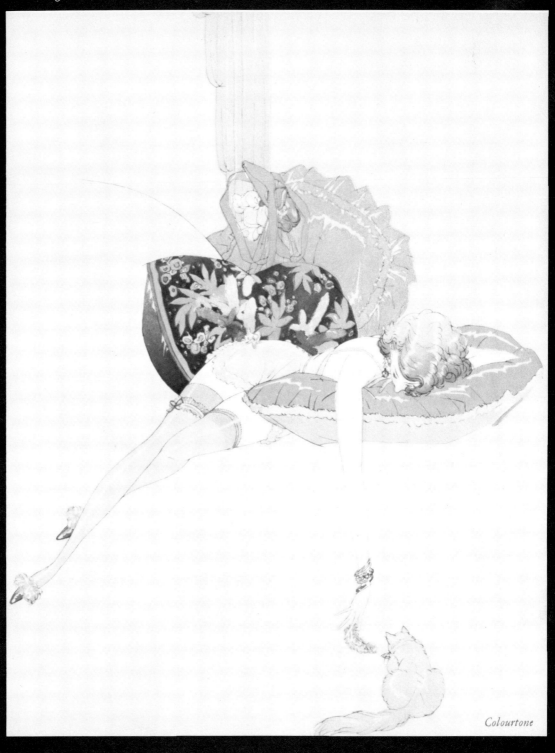

Colourtone

A "Varga Girl," February, 1944.

NOVEMBER

November's swell for hunting—
But this year it seems flat!
The only men worth hunting for
Are hunting for a rat!

S	M	T	W	T	F	S
	1	2	3	4	5	6
7	8	9	10	11	12	13
14	☠	16	17	18	19	20
21	22	23	24	25	26	27
28	29	30				

A *"Varga Girl,"* November, 1943.

ARTISTS SKETCH PAD CALENDAR, 1957. This was one of Brown & Bigelow's responses to the great success of the Varga pinup calendar and PLAYBOY's ever-popular Playmate calendars. Using an updated concept of an art calendar being an acceptable vehicle for presenting sexy women, B & B ran a series of "Artist Sketch Pad" calendars, each page containing a color pinup and secondary pseudoacademic "figure studies" in the background. Still more conservative than its competition, the Sketch Pad Calendar style was painterly and even arty. Artist: Withers. Size: 9" × 11½".

Good? It's perfect!

APRIL

Sun	Mon	Tue	Wed	Thu	Fri	Sat
·	1	2	3	4	5	6
7	8	9	10	11	12	13
14	15	16	17	18	19	20
21	22	23	24	25	26	27
28	29	30	·	·	·	·

THEODORE BOGNER AND SONS, Inc.
General Contractors
Commercial Building and Repair
P. O. Box 134 - WOOSTER, OHIO
Phone 2-6730

In this 1965 "Artist Sketch Pad," the pose is as sexy as the photographic styles in PLAYBOY and other magazines. The art itself, by the well-known Fritz Willis, is quite realistic, yet the sketchbook format seems to detract from the eroticism of the model. Size: 8½" × 12". Courtesy Brown & Bigelow.

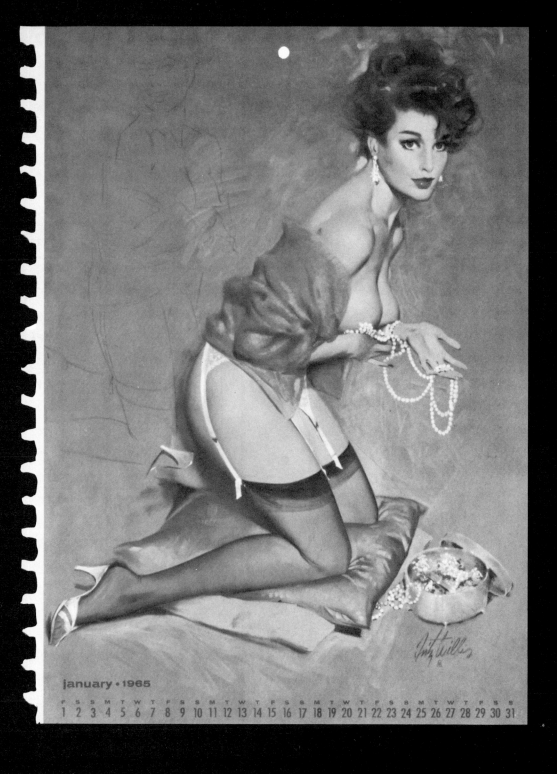

january • 1965

F S S M T W T F S S M T W T F S S M T W T F S S M T W T F S S
1 2 3 4 5 6 7 8 9 10 11 12 13 14 15 16 17 18 19 20 21 22 23 24 25 26 27 28 29 30 31

Rolf Armstrong was undoubtedly one of America's finest creators of "girl" art. He worked only from living models, not photographs, as so many other artists did. Right: Armstrong and Jewel Flower, his most-often-used model, who posed for the calendars on these two pages. According to Armstrong, Jewel was "unspoiled, charming, spontaneous, and enthusiastic . . . with features, physical charms and the joy of life of the true American beauty." Below: "Let's Go," a 1941 calendar. Far Right: "That's A Deal," a 1949 calendar pinup. Courtesy Brown & Bigelow.

BROWN & BIGELOW
SAINT PAUL 4, MINNESOTA

Following the contemporary poster boom in the late 1960s, the "Soulmate" calendar for 1971 was published and distributed through retail stores. All twelve pictures feature chic black models who are refreshingly brash in the satirical photographs on civil-rights themes. Shown here is the "pickaninny" theme. (See also the unflattering version on page 39.) Other subjects included takeoffs on Betsy Ross, soul food, the Civil War, minstrels, slavery, the Ku Klux Klan, and the Statue of Liberty. The calendar did not sell well, according to the publisher, because it was too sophisticated for both blacks and whites in mass-market areas. It was most appreciated by a liberal (if not radical) minority who unfortunately were not interested in buying the calendar. Size: 14" × 15". Published by Poster Prints, Norristown, Pa.

1939 MARCH 1939

SUN.	MON.	TUE.	WED.	THU.	FRI.	SAT.
			1	2	3	4
5	6	7	8	9	10	11
12	13	14	15	16	17	18
19	20	21	22	23	24	25
26	27	28	29	30	31	

APRIL 1939

1939 MAY 1939

SUN.	MON.	TUE.	WED.	THU.	FRI.	SAT.
	1	2	3	4	5	6
7	8	9	10	11	12	13
14	15	16	17	18	19	20
21	22	23	24	25	26	27
28	29	30	31			

SUN	MON	TUE	WED	THUR	FRI	SAT

Don't Suffer **NEEDLESS PAIN**

Try **DR. MILES ANTI-PAIN PILLS**
FOR HEADACHES, NEURALGIA AND MUSCULAR PAINS

APRIL PLANTING DATES
1-2—Unfavorable for planting or transplanting. Good time to destroy weeds. 3-4—Good for flowers. Not good for other crops. 5-6-7—Good for pulp and roots. 8-9—Good for all crops. 10-11—Unfavorable for planting. 12-13-14—Good for stalks and roots. 15-16—Seeds planted now likely to rot. 17-18-19—Good for all crops. 20-21—Fairly good for crops that yield above ground. 22-23—Fine time to plant root crops. 24-25—Favorable for plants which yield above ground. 28-29-30—Unfavorable for planting or transplanting. Good time to destroy weeds.

Sunrise 5:43; Sets 6:24
1 FAIR — Sets 4:01 a.m.

Sunrise 5:42; Sets 6:25
2 PALM SUNDAY — FAIR — Sets 4:36 a.m.

Sunrise 5:40; Sets 6:26
3 COOL — Rises 6:10 p.m. Full Moon

Sunrise 5:39; Sets 6:28
4 CHANGEABLE — Rises 7:19 p.m.

Sunrise 5:37; Sets 6:29
5 SHOWERS — Rises 8:28 p.m.

Sunrise 5:36; Sets 6:30
6 SHOWERS — Rises 9:31 p.m.

Sunrise 5:35; Sets 6:31
7 GOOD FRI. — CLOUDY — Rises 10:32 p.m.

Sunrise 5:33; Sets 6:32
8 CLEAR — Rises 11:28 p.m.

Sunrise 5:31; Sets 6:33
9 EASTER — WARM — Rises Morn.

Sunrise 5:30; Sets 6:34
10 WARM — Rises 0:18 a.m.

Sunrise 5:28; Sets 6:35
11 FAIR — Rises 0:58 a.m. Last Quarter

Sunrise 5:27; Sets 6:36
12 FAIR — Rises 1:39 a.m.

Sunrise 5:25; Sets 6:37
13 CLOUDY — Rises 2:13 a.m.

Sunrise 5:23; Sets 6:38
14 SHOWERS — Rises 2:44 a.m.

Sunrise 5:22; Sets 6:39
15 SHOWERS — Rises 3:14 a.m.

Sunrise 5:20; Sets 6:40
16 LOW SUN. — STORMY — Rises 3:43 a.m.

Sunrise 5:19; Sets 6:41
17 COOL — Rises 4:09 a.m.

Sunrise 5:17; Sets 6:42
18 COOL — Rises 4:40 a.m.

Sunrise 5:16; Sets 6:43
19 WARM — Sets 6:56 p.m. New Moon

Sunrise 5:14; Sets 6:44
20 WARM — Sets 8:00 p.m.

Sunrise 5:13; Sets 6:45
21 PLEASANT — Sets 9:03 p.m.

Sunrise 5:12; Sets 6:46
22 FAIR — Sets 10:04 p.m.

2nd Sunday after Easter
23 Sets 11:01 p.m. / **30** 3rd Sunday after Easter — Sets 3:10 a.m.

Sunrise 5:09; Sets 6:48
24 FAIR — Rises 11:54 p.m.

Sunrise 5:07; Sets 6:49
25 FOGGY — Sets Morn.

Sunrise 5:06; Sets 6:50
26 UNSETTLED — Sets 0:41 a.m. First Quarter

Sunrise 5:04; Sets 6:51
27 SHOWERY — Sets 1:23 a.m.

Sunrise 5:03; Sets 6:52
28 DAMP — Sets 2:02 a.m.

Sunrise 5:02; Sets 6:53
29 DAMP — Sets 2:36 a.m.

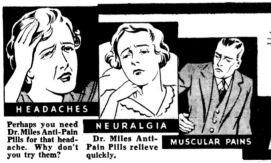

WEATHER FORECAST—1st to 3rd—Fair Wave. Fair and cool in states east of the Rocky Mountains. Warm in states of the Gulf coast. 4th to 9th—Changeable. Thunder storms over the south. Rain over Middle Atlantic and New England states. Threatening over states of the northwest. 10th to 13th—Warm Wave. Clear in New England and Middle Atlantic states. Showers in states of the southwest and the Gulf border. 14th to 16th—Stormy. Gales along Lake border and states of the northwest. Threatening over middlewest. Rain in southern and eastern portions. 17th to 21st—Cool Spell. Pleasant in states of the south and southwest. Cool in the Rocky Mountain region and the middlewest. 22nd to 25th—Fair Period. Seasonable conditions at most points east of the Rocky Mountains. Damp and foggy in states of the Atlantic slope. 26th to 30th—Cloudy Spell. Cloudy and showery over Lake region, Middle Atlantic and New England states. Unsettled over southwest sections. Wind along Pacific coast waters.

A typical drugstore calendar from 1939, advertising "Dr. Miles" pharmaceutical products. Calendars of this type were distributed to pharmacies, drugstores, and chemists. A great deal of information was included: planting dates, daily weather forecasts, phases of the moon, and monthly weather predictions. The illustrations are in the style of the cheap pulp publications of the 1930s. Artist unidentified. Size: 9½" × 12½".

Lawson Wood began illustrating for Brown & Bigelow in 1932. He introduced to millions of people an anthropomorphized chimpanzee family headed by "Gran'pop," in a satirical series concerned with American stereotypes. Right: In this 1945 calendar we see Gran'pop, "The Expert," as the prognosticator. The humor here is in the chart behind Gran pop showing "next year" and "next month" crossed out and "well, tomorrow" still applicable to the accuracy of his predictions. Below: "A Proud Pauper," 1950.

Wood was English—he refused many handsome offers to reside and work in the United States—yet his illustrations were uncannily in the American vernacular. Wood's calendars have been popular equally with children and adults, and have retained a timelessness that has allowed Brown & Bigelow to reissue even his earliest artwork for over four decades.

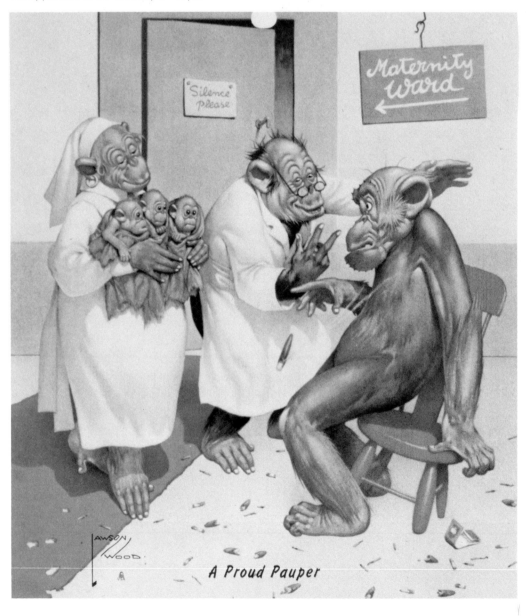

A Proud Pauper

"THE EXPERT"

An English calendar by David Weston, an artist with a special knack for recreating nostalgia from the early days of technology. Weston was discovered by Eversheds, the calendar publisher, quite by accident, when an elderly couple wrote a letter to the London DAILY EXPRESS requesting a picture of an early locomotive. Weston responded, the picture was published, and then adapted by Eversheds as a calendar. Since that time (around 1973), Weston has had steady work and a soaring reputation as an English artist. Size: 11" × 19". Courtesy Eversheds Ltd., St. Albans.

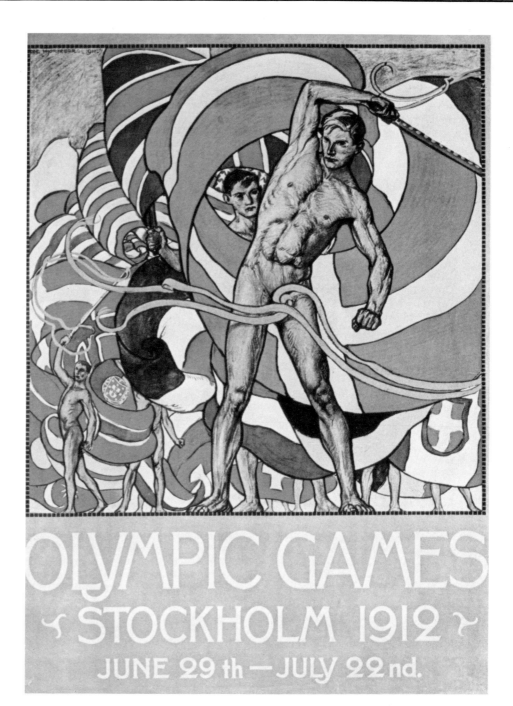

The Olympia Kalendar for 1972, published in Holland, with a date pad printed in German, French, and English. The calendar features the thirteen original posters from the Olympics, from 1912 to 1972. Size: 10" × 17½". Published by Antik Print, Amsterdam.

Following page:
Guillermo Mordillo calendar for 1975, published by Top Present, one of Germany's newest and most contemporary calendar companies. Mordillo produces several multilingual calendars annually, all quite successful on the retail market. The example shown here is from "Happy Mordillo," in a style that might be described as fantasy cartoons. Mordillo is a native of Argentina who resides in Paris. Size: 16" × 11". Courtesy Top Present, Munich.